T0157036

REJECTING OFFENSE,
STRIFE, AND UNFORGIVENESS

REJECTING OFFENSE, STRIFE, AND UNFORGIVENESS

Rediscovering the Use of the Tongue

Samuel Kioko Kiema

REJECTING OFFENSE, STRIFE, AND UNFORGIVENESS
REDISCOVERING THE USE OF THE TONGUE

iUniverse books may be ordered through booksellers or by contacting:

iUniverse
1663 Liberty Drive
Bloomington, IN 47403
www.iuniverse.com
1-800-Authors (1-800-288-4677)

ISBN: 978-1-4917-9984-0 (sc)
ISBN: 978-1-4917-9985-7 (e)

Library of Congress Control Number: 2016914583

Print information available on the last page.

iUniverse rev. date: 10/12/2016

Contents

Introduction

We pray this book will help our readers to understand that Bitter envy, Strife, Offense, and Unforgiveness are impediments that stop them from fulfilling God's will and purpose concerning the whole duty of humankind. Our goal is to help them grow through dedicated and practical teachings from the word of God. We intend to help Christians thrive in their walks by providing empowering knowledge to nourish and cherish one another in healthy relationships. We believe the Spirit of God has disclosed the mind of God relative to living victorious lives by coming into agreement and bringing forth His kingdom and creating His will in the earth as it is in heaven. It is to the readers benefit to understand that the Father desires for them to reflect His order and dominion in the earth. This will occur by avoiding strife and envy that bring offense and by forgiving transgressors. The Father wants people's lives on earth to be triumphant and victorious, operating in the wisdom that comes from above, because it is first pure and then peaceable, gentle, willing to yield, full of mercy and good fruits, without partiality, and without hypocrisy.

Acknowledgements

First, to my Lord and Savior, Jesus Christ, who has prepared and anointed me to herald His gospel. I am honored to be charged with such a responsibility. I am forever grateful for His perpetual grace upon my life so that I may make known the power of His gospel. Thank You, Lord, for delighting in the prosperity of Your servant. I declare my best days are with me, speaking blessing, favor, increase, and multiplication into my tomorrow. I call You Lord.

To my beautiful, excellent, godly wife; my intimate and covenant friend, the love of my life; and my co-worker in God's purpose, Jedidah, who continues to show me the joy of life. I thank the Lord for such a perfect match for my strengths and weaknesses. The trust you have in my ability to see and hear from God causes me to walk in a deeper level of fear of the Lord. I thank you for your chaste conduct accompanied with godly fear and for sharing this work with me and encouraging me to do all that God has assigned us. You are the most profound representation of Jesus I have ever known. Your walk of love, humility, forgiveness, gentleness, and faith challenge me daily. I thank you for being a loving mother to our three children, Faith, Susan, and Samuel Jr., whom you have helped to raise in the fear of the Lord. I thank you for believing the gift of God in me and requesting that I write this book. What a treasure and jewel you are to me. You are my world, my sunshine, my precious gift from the Father. Through you I have obtained favor with the Lord. Thank you for trusting me to lead you into the purposes of God. My world revolves around you.

To my bishop, apostle, and prophetic friend, Bishop Clarence E. McClendon of Full Harvest International Church and of Clarence E. McClendon Ministries, who helped father me into the service of our Lord Jesus Christ to connect people to the power of God. Thank you for prophesying to my destiny, preaching revelatory rhema word, teaching, and training me how to speak God's Word to situations that speak contrary to my destiny, how to pray the word of God and get results, how to hear the voice of God, and how to discern and respond to issues knowing that the issue is never the issue in the situation. You helped develop the gifts of God in me. I honor you.

To my mother, Martha, who helped raise me in the fear of God amid destitution and impoverishment and believed in hope against hope, that I would become a blessing, knowing that I was called to this, that I may inherit a blessing and would become a blessing to others. I am blessed by your strength and your example of humility. You discerned the gift of God in me and helped to develop it. I call you blessed.

To the faithful, trustworthy covenant friends Josephine and Eric Mwania, Reverend Jane Wanjiku, Michael and Rania Isaac, Dorcas Wanjohi, Helen Mbaabu, Glen and Kaby Lett, Boniface Tsobnang, Ramaiah and Lily Samuel, Ben ha and Wasuki, Ann Marie Karkow, Melvin and Adalina, and my sister Emily Ngulutu, whom the Lord has connected to the anointing in my life as I seek to connect people to the kingdom of

God and equip the saints for the work of the ministry, establishing them in the foundation of God that stands sure. Thank you for encouraging my faith and strengthening me in the things of God by supplying for the Great Commission to prepare people to enter into the kingdom of our Lord. I pray for you that the Lord, who supplies seed to the sower and bread for food, supplies and multiplies the seed you have sown and increases the fruits of your righteousness, and that enriched in everything for all liberality, which causes thanksgiving through us to God. I call you partners in the Lord's business.

To my daughters, Faith-Kiema Phillips and Susan-Kiema; my son, Samuel K. Kiema Jr.; my sons in-law, Seilas Phillips and Michael Adams; and my grandchildren, Solomon, Zoe, Drusilla, and Zion. I thank you for your support and maturity in releasing me to fulfill the great call in my life. The Lord bless you on credit as you grow to maturity in the things of God. You are my earthly inheritance.

1

REDISCOVERING THE USE OF THE TONGUE

Tongue abuse perpetuates offense and strife. The tongue has the ability to turn a situation, ministry organization, business organization, household, relationship, family, or marriage around, either for the worse by strife or for the better by God's Word. When Strife, Envy, Offense, and Unforgiveness are permitted in one's life, it makes one unable to say, "We have Done What was our Duty to do".

Before we can go further with speaking about rediscovering the use of the tongue, let us first deal with offense and strife to have an understanding of how they are perpetuated. Jesus Christ dealt with it in detail and warned the disciples in Luke 17:1 that "It is impossible that no offenses should come, but woe to him through whom they do come!" In Luke 17:10, Jesus Christ tells the disciples "likewise you, when you have done all those things which you are commanded, say, 'We are unprofitable servants. We have done what was our duty to do."

Jesus the Christ implores His followers to do all the good they can, by all the means they can, in all the ways they can, in all the places they can, at all the times they can, to all the people they can, and as long as ever they can to avoid bitter envy, strife, offense, unforgiveness, confusion, and all kinds of evil works. Then He said to the disciples in Luke 17:1, "It is impossible that no offenses should come, but woe to him through whom they do come!"

Jesus used the word *offense* to warn us about events that transpire in life with the potential to trap up us so that we may fail to fulfill our whole man's duty.

If you are going to deal with bitter envy and strife in its totality, it is conditional that you also must deal with "offense" and "unforgiveness" "Offense" is one of the components that produces strife and divisions among people of destiny. When we speak of "strife", we are addressing contentions, disagreements, divisions, divide and rule attitudes. This is not to be named among people of destiny, but it must be stopped.

Christians, we must understand that as much as we are kings, priests, sons, and heirs in the kingdom of God, we are also servants, ambassadors, and representatives of Christ, in the earth, endeavoring to accomplish a mission that has been committed to our care: of reconciling men to God. Therefore, as workers and laborers together with Christ, we have a duty to fulfill. We are to fulfill our duty differently from other people who do not live by Bible's faith. When we deal with offense, strife, and unforgiveness as Christ instructed, it will pave the way not only for harvesting of souls, but also for healing of relationships, diseases, infirmities, souls, and the land. We will be able to do all those things that have been commanded of us to do. And on that great and notable day of the Lord, we will stand before Him, who is and who was and who is to come and confidently say, "We have done what was our duty to do."

In the book of Ecclesiastes 12:13, Solomon gives us a summary of all that God requires of mankind "Let us hear the conclusion of the whole matter: Fear God, and keep his commandments: for this is the whole duty of man."

The above statement refers to the whole of what is contained in the word of God. The preacher calls upon himself, as well as his hearers, to attend to fearing God and keeping His commandments. "The fear of God" and "keeping of the commandments," or obedience to the whole will of God, is the fruit, effect, and evidence of the former dispensation and takes in all the commands of God, both moral and positive, whether under the former or present dispensation. Observance of the fear of God and "keeping of His commandments" in faith from a principle of love, position of finished work, and with a view to the glory of God is the whole {duty} of mankind. "The fear of God" and "keeping of His commandments" is what makes a person whole, perfect, and wanting nothing.

Without "the fear of God" and "keeping His commandments", a person is nothing. He or she may possess so much of the wisdom, wealth, honor, and profits of this world, but without this fear of God, the person is nothing. "This is the whole of every person", as we supply it, the duty, work, and business of every man of every son of Abraham, be he or she, what he or she will, high or low, rich or poor, of every age, gender, and condition. This is the happiness of every man, or that it leads to it. This is the whole of it.

Chapter 2

CHRISTIANITY HAS BOTH PRIVILEGES AND DUTY OR RESPONSIBILITY

Our modern Christianity is deemed to have privileges only and no responsibility whatsoever. Modern day Christians don't understand that the other side of privileges is responsibility or duty. Now we have Christians who want privileges, access, power, visibility, influence, fame, notoriety, and no responsibility. They fail to understand that they have a responsibility and duty as Christians. These things they want come with great responsibilities and a price to pay, some cost, and with opportunity cost. Jesus said in Luke 17:1 that, "It is impossible but that offences will come." That means, as a disciple of Jesus Christ, sometimes somebody will offend you.

But what is an offense?" The word "*offense*" comes from the Greek word *skandalon*, from which we get the word *scandal*. The word *offense* means a trigger to the trap. The word *strife* means a trap. This is a powerful picture that you must understand! The word *skandalon* (Trigger) originally described the small piece of wood that was used to keep the door of an animal trap propped open. A piece of food was placed inside the trap to lure the animal inside. When the animal entered the trap and accidentally bumped the skandalon (Trigger), or the small piece of wood, the skandalon (Trigger) collapsed, causing the trap door to slam shut and the animal to be caught inside with no way to escape.

However, the New Testament also uses the word *skandalon (Trigger)* to refer to a stone or an obstacle that causes one to trip, to stumble, to lose his footing, to waver, to falter, and to fall down. In 1 Peter 2:8, the word *skandalon* is used to describe how unbelievers react to the Gospel when they don't want to hear it or believe it. Peter said, "And a stone of stumbling, and a rock of offence, even to them which stumble at the word", Rather than accept the message and be saved, these people stumble when they hear the truth, tripping over the message that could set them free.

But in Luke 17:1, Jesus used the word *skandalon* to warn us about events that happen in life with the potential to trap us up. Sometimes Satan baits us with something, drawing us into a trap in which he knows we will become offended. When we bump into a moment of offense, the trap slams down shut, and like an animal that is trapped in a cage and can't get out, we suddenly find ourselves caught in a miserable situation, trapped in detrimental and negative emotions!

An offense usually occurs when you see, hear, or experience a behavior that is different from what you expected, and that causes you to falter, totter, and wobble in your soul. In fact, you are so stunned by what you have observed or by a failed expectation that you lose your footing emotionally. Before you know it, you are dumbfounded and flabbergasted about something. Then your shock turns into disbelief, your disbelief turns into disappointment, and your disappointment turns into offense. When this happens, you will hear people say things like, "I can't believe he or she did that."

We all have experienced this kind of disappointment at some point in our lives, and according to Jesus's words in Luke 17:1, "It is impossible but that offences will come."

3

OBJECTIVE OF OFFENSE

The objective of offense (trigger, bait) is to trap you; it is literally to make you take the bait. The offense is not the trap, but the trigger or bait to the trap. The offense is meant to trigger something else. Offense is sent to you or released your way to trigger something else. Offense is not the important issue, but what comes after is the issue. What comes after the offense (trigger) is what the devil is after and wants to happen. Jesus warned of offenses and said in Matthew 18:6, "Whoever causes one of these little ones who believe in Me to sin, it would be better for him if a millstone were hung around his neck, and he were drowned in the depth of the sea."

The opportunity to be offended comes to each of us. As long as we live and breathe, we must combat this nuisance and refuse to allow it to have a place in our hearts and minds. Even worse, we have all been the source of offense at some point or another. It may not have been intentional on our part; in fact, we may not even know we offended anyone until someone later informs us of what we did.

The offense is the bait. A fish goes after the bait, not the hook. The fish does not see the hook, but, the trigger. We get the demonic attack because we took the bait. Our minds cannot rest because we took the bait. We take the bait because we do not discern or see the hook. The scripture is telling us the trap is the hook.

If you are born again, you must know why you are to walk away from the offense. You just have to leave an offense alone; it doesn't matter who is right. It doesn't matter whether you have been wronged, please don't take the bait. Do all the good you can, by all the means you can, in all the ways you can, in all the places you can, at all the times you can, to all the people you can. as long as you can to avoid offense.

We must learn to do our best and avoid being a source of offense to anyone. At the same time, do not be shocked if you find out that someone somewhere has been offended. In Luke 17:1 Jesus told His apostles they would have opportunities to take the bait because the enemy would plant seeds of discord among people because they come from different backgrounds, wake up in bad moods, have a bad day at work, don't physically feel well, and go through a whole host of other negative experiences in their lives. Their interpretation of our actions and words may be very different from the original intention.

Offense is a Promise, not a Prophesy

Your brothers and sisters in church and at home are capable of offending you. When you are not informed, you will be offended in church, and you will say things like, "I can't believe I got offended in church!" "I can't believe my spouse offended me!" "I can't believe my family offended me!" Well, why can't you believe it? Jesus said it, and it must be so. Jesus said, "It is impossible, but that offences will come." This was a promise and not a prophesy.

Christians everywhere come to the house of God to hear His word, and whether or not they consciously know it, they are being transformed by the renewing of their minds by God's word. They have not been completely renewed in their minds yet. They are potential offenders, and therefore they will offend you.

Woe to Him through Whom Offenses Come

Jesus addressed the seriousness of offenses and, said in Luke 17:1b-2 "But woe to him through whom offenses come! It would be better for him if a millstone were hung around his neck, and he were thrown into the sea, than that he should offend one of these little ones." Jesus takes offenses seriously when it is perpetrated against one of His children. If you are one of His children, then you must avoid offending His other children.

When you are offended, however, Jesus articulated four considerations that you are to be responsible for in Luke 17:3–4. "[3]Take heed to yourselves. If your brother sins against you, rebuke him; and if he repents, forgive him. [4]And if he sins against you seven times in a day, and seven times in a day returns to you, saying, 'I repent,' you shall forgive him." In verse 3 Jesus begins instruction on offenses. The instruction on offense is to the offended, not to the offender. This immediately alters our perception on offense. When we get offended, all the attention goes to the offender contrary to what Jesus teaches.

Because offense is something that is going to happen, it is wise to prepare for it. Examples of preparation for something which must happen in the future would be when you are going to travel and prepare for the journey, when a woman is pregnant, and prepares for the baby's arrival, when you are a candidate and prepare for the test and job interview, and when you want to build a house and prepare for its construction. When you know something is going to come, you prepare for it. Therefore because we all live in an offense zone, we need to know how to deal with it. If you don't know how to deal with offense, chances are you will be contributing to the strife, bitter envy, confusion, and all kinds of evil works, and demonic attacks.

Take Heed to Yourselves

When you are offended, the first thing Jesus said you are to do is "take heed to yourselves." When you get offended, your first responsibility is not to the offender, but to take heed to yourself. It means paying attention to yourself. This is too important **not** to take notice of. Please recognize the purpose of the offense. Why is the offense coming? Because we now know the word *offense* means a trigger on a trap, and so the offense is a trigger that is supposed to start a trap in your life. Offense is a trigger that is designed to close you in, close you off, and shut you down. That is why Jesus is saying take heed to yourself, because whatever it is that is coming is designed to trap you. It is a trap for you, not for the offender. Therefore when you know that offense is a trap for you, it changes the way you respond to it.

Who Shall Offend You?

Anyone whom you don't have a relationship with cannot offend you. The only people who can offend you are the ones with whom you have a relationship. Therefore do not be surprised when people who are close to you offend you. These are the only people who can offend you. In Luke 17:3, Jesus said to the apostles, "Take heed to yourselves if your brother sins against you". Paul, writing to the Church in Rome, admonishes them in Romans 14:21. "It is good neither to eat meat nor drink wine nor do anything by which YOUR BROTHER stumbles or is offended or is made weak."

Notice that they are both referring to "your brother", someone with whom you have a relationship. That helps you narrow down the people who can offend you: Your spouse, parents, children, family, people in church, friends, business partners, employees, employers, students, educators and work mates. Anybody you have a relationship with is a potential offender, except for those who have the wisdom that comes from above. When a fool acts like a fool, that does not bother me, but when someone who is supposed to be responsible, intelligent, and caring acts like a fool, that bothers me. Why is that? Because I am expecting something different from them. The same is true when somebody in the household of faith acts contrary to expectations. When you have expectations of people to function in a certain way, and they don't, that is when you get offended. Jesus says when that happens, take your eyes off them because it is no longer about them. This is now about you. Recognize what it is: a trap. I don't know about you, but that changes the game for me. When I know you are trying to trap me, that changes everything. When I understand you want to shut me down, that changes everything. I cannot afford to let anybody shut me down, so at this point I have to pay attention to myself. What happens to you is between you and Jesus. You are the culprit, but I am paying attention to myself.

4

ALL OFFENSE IS NOT A VIOLATION OF GOD'S SPIRITUAL LAW

In Luke 17:3, Jesus said, "If your brother sins against you, (misses the mark) and repents, forgive him." The word *sin* in this context does not mean that you have violated a spiritual law; It means someone has missed the mark that you set for them. In 1 Corinthians 8:13, [13]Paul states, "if meat makes my brother stumble, I will never again eat meat, lest I make my brother stumble." When people offend us, we immediately think that they have violated God's law. Everybody who offends you has not violated God's law. Most of the people who offend you have simply fallen short of the mark you set for them. This is another reason why Jesus said you should pay attention to yourself, because you may have set a mark that is unrealistic.

Proverbs 25:19 states, "[19]Confidence in an unfaithful man in time of trouble Is like a bad tooth and a foot out of joint." You may be expecting people to fly like eagles when they have never possessed wings. Sometimes our expectations for our fellow brothers and sisters are unrealistic. They do not miss God's mark for them, but they miss our mark for them. We should have God's expectations for others.

People may violate your personal space by getting too close, and they may offend you with bad breath or sweaty stench. Your expectation for them is to brush their teeth after every meal. Expectation of them is to visit their dentist every six months to have their teeth cleaned up. Your expectation for them is to take a shower or bath every day, especially when they are coming to the house of God, is to use deodorant and perfumes on themselves. If these expectations are not met, they may actually get you offended and impede your ability to receive God's word. This is an extreme example of violation of nonspiritual law, however this person may actually offend you because they did not meet your expectations for personal hygiene. They did not violate God's spiritual law, like adultery or stealing. You keep wondering, "Can't they smell themselves?" It is important that you distinguish between the mark God has set and the mark you have set.

If you are honest with yourself, you will soon realize that something that offends you shouldn't offend you. A sign of spiritual maturity is when you stop getting offended by things that used to offend you. People who are constantly offended by things are juveniles and and they are to grow up.

Luke 17:3 Says ……. "If your brother sins against you, rebuke him." The word *rebuke* in this context does not mean that you get angry, and start throwing punches. The word rebuke means, "Stop it that is enough." By the word of God, we understand that in the kingdom of God, we are to speak the truth in love.

Ephesians 4:14–15 states that "we should no longer be children, tossed to and fro and carried about with every wind of doctrine, by the trickery of men, in the cunning craftiness of deceitful plotting, [15]but, speaking the truth in love, may grow up in all things into Him who is the head—Christ [16]from whom the whole body, is joined and knit together by what every joint supplies, according to the effective working by which every part does its share, causes growth of the body for the edifying of itself in love."

Proverbs 25:15 says "By long forbearance a ruler is persuaded, And a gentle tongue breaks a bone."

Just because you are offended, that is not a justification to get ugly when you deal with your brother or sister. Please note that Jesus puts the responsibility of initiating the conversation on the offended, not the offender. The offended party is the one with the responsibility to communicate. The people who offend you may not even know that they have offended you. The offended party casts down strife by initiating communication with the offender. Communication with the offender does not allow wounds to fester unchecked. It does not allow people to be wounded and not communicate, but you have to be mature regarding how to communicate. If we people spoke truth in love with one another, you will find that the person who offended you is unaware.

In Matthew 15:10–14, Jesus says, "Hear and understand:Not what goes into the mouth defiles a man; but what comes out of the mouth, this defiles a man. Then His disciples came and said to Him, 'Do You know that the Pharisees were offended when they heard this saying?' [13]But He answered and said, 'Every plant which My heavenly Father has not planted will be uprooted. [14]Let them alone. They are blind leaders of the blind. And if the blind leads the blind, both will fall into a ditch.'"

If offence arises from the statement of the truth, it is more expedient that the offence be permitted to arise than that the truth should be abandoned.

Assume Your Christian Responsibility

The second instruction Jesus gave when offense comes is that you should assume your Christian responsibility. In an offended situation, you are to assume your Christian responsibility. Your Christian responsibility is to your brother or sister who offended you, and you should reconcile. You should not gossip about them to a third party. The first thing we ought to do when a saved Christian comes to us with an accusation is to examine ourselves. The scripture in 2 Corinthians 13:5 encourages us to "Examine yourselves as to whether you are in the faith. Test yourselves. Know for yourselves, that Jesus Christ is in you—unless indeed you are disqualified."

When the Bible speaks of offense, it refers primarily to some act or series of acts that lead another into sin. By themselves, offenses are generally not hurt feelings, resentment, and anger that begin as minor irritations or annoyances. We ought to be able to deal easily with these. However, irritations and annoyances have the unfortunate inclination to build into far worse bitterness and grudges, which are sins that a person has allowed himself to be led into—in many cases by his own devious mind.

We don't have a responsibility to other Christians to examine ourselves any more than we have a responsibility to other Christians to study the word of God. Our responsibility is to the Lord Jesus Christ.

2 Timothy 2:15 tells us to "Study to show ourselves approved unto God workmen that need not to be ashamed, rightly dividing the word of truth."

Christians, we are to show ourselves approved unto God by turning others over whom we possess influence from the pursuit of vain and unprofitable things. Then our work will be the work of workmen tested by trial, and it will have stood the test. Literally, the offended is to be zealous, make haste, or diligently endeavor to present yourself approved to God, whatever men may judge of you and your services. As a workman who needs not to be ashamed either on account of unfaithfulness, ignorance, lukewarmness, negligence, or sloth, but you are to rightly cut up the word. Those disposed to strife, will commonly strive about matters of small moments. But strife of words destroy the things of God.

If offence arises from the statement of the truth, it is more expedient that offense be permitted to arise than that the truth should be abandoned. There is nothing more offensive to hypocrites than pressing spiritual worship and allegiance to God and belittling external rituals and actions not attended with a suitable inward respect and devotion of heart.

Be Ready to Forgive

When you are offended the third thing Jesus said you are to do is "Be ready to forgive." Actually, you should be able to forgive people before you get to them. That is to say you are to release forgiveness toward the offender. Notice that forgiveness is something to be done by faith. In Luke 17:5, the apostles said to the Lord, "Increase our faith." The appeal for faith was not for moving mountains, working miracles, or healing diseases, but it was about forgiveness. It was FAITH to forgive. Real forgiveness is a walk of faith. Don't say that you have faith and yet you are always offended.

Jesus our Lord says in Matthew 5:43-48, [43]"You have heard that it was said, 'You shall love your neighbor[a] and hate your enemy.' [44]But I say to you, **(1)** love your enemies**, (2)** bless those who curse you, **(3)** do good to those who hate you, and **(4)** pray for those who spitefully use you and persecute you, [45] that you may be sons of your Father in heaven; for He makes His sun rise on the evil and on the good, and sends rain on the just and on the unjust. [46]For if you love those who love you, what reward have you? Do not even the tax collectors do the same? [47]And if you greet your brethren only, what do you do more than others? Do not even the tax collectors[d] do so? [48]Therefore you shall be perfect, just as your Father in heaven is perfect."

In Proverbs 25:21-22, Solomon commands, "[21]If your enemy is hungry, give him bread to eat; And if he is thirsty, give him water to drink; [22]For so you will heap coals of fire on his head, And the LORD will reward you."

Walk It by Faith

The fourth thing Jesus said you are to do when you are offended is "Walk it by faith." Walking in forgiveness is a faith walk; it requires faith to forgive. Forgiveness requires speaking what you believe God has said regarding forgiveness. In order to forgive, you have to speak or release something toward somebody.

In Luke 17:5, the apostles said to the Lord, "Increase our faith." When Jesus warned the apostles on offenses they realized they didn't possess faith; the kind of faith that is required to deal with the offense and forgiveness. They understood that they needed their faith increased, in order to be able to forgive offenses. We know that faith is persuasion or conviction plus corresponding action. In other words, you are persuaded or convinced that it is God's will and commandment not to receive offense or offend, but to forgive. The corresponding actions to this persuasion or belief is speaking and doing what God has said concerning the offense and forgiveness. Jesus said in Matthew 5:44 that whenever someone offends you, deal with the offense from four fronts. (1) "Love them, (2) Bless them, (3) Do good to them, and (4) Pray for them."

What Jesus meant in Matthew 5:45 is that you become the sons of your Father in heaven when you love, bless, do good, and pray for someone who has offended you. Your Father in heaven uses His faith to do everything He does. You become your Father's son by walking by faith. He fathered you into this world, but you become His son by doing His commandments. In honor of the Father, an obedient son does only what he sees His father do. Forgiveness is realized by loving, blessing, doing good, and praying by faith for someone who has offended you. When you speak and declare the word of God relative to the situation, you get to the posture of love, blessing, doing good, and praying for someone who has offended you, regard less of what you feel, hear, see, smell, or taste. It is not a sensory matter, but a faith matter.

While instructing the apostles, Jesus said in Luke 17:6, "If you have faith as a mustard seed, you can say to this mulberry tree, Be pulled up by the roots and be planted in the sea, and it would obey you." Your faith is released when you say something about forgiveness. If you are going to forgive, you have to say or declare something about forgiveness.

Paul said in Romans 10:10, "10 For with the heart one believes unto righteousness, and with the mouth confession is made unto salvation." Forgiveness is not something you do with your heart, but with your mouth. If you believe it is your responsibility to forgive, you must say so.

Your Faith Will Obey You.

Luke 17:6 Jesus said, "It would obey you," which is indicative. It is referring to FAITH, not the mulberry tree. The subject here is your faith. Your faith will obey you. The tree has no responsibility to obey you, but faith does.

Luke 17:7-9 says "[7]And which of you, having a servant plowing or tending sheep, will say to him when he has come in from the field, 'Come at once and sit down to eat'? [8]But will he not rather say to him, 'Prepare something for my supper, and gird yourself and serve me, till I have eaten and drunk, and afterward you will eat and drink'? [9]Does he thank that servant because he did the things that were commanded him? I think not."

Our Lord Jesus is making a comparison of your faith to your servant. If you perpetually speak to your faith, it will obey you in the same manner a servant would his master. If you repeatedly say, "I forgive them," your faith will cause forgiveness to come to pass. It is a faith matter, not a sensory one. If you have to do it seven times a day, it is worth it. Do not change your confession about your brother or your sister. When feelings of bitterness, strife, envy, and confusion speak to you, speak out to them, "I have forgiven them." Tell the feelings, "No! I have forgiven them." Tell the strife, "No! I have forgiven them." Tell the bitter envy "No I have forgiven them. Tell the confusion "No I have forgiven them." Jesus says if you keep on speaking, your faith, it will obey you. Your faith will drive out strife, envy, confusion, and all evil work.

chapter

5

WE HAVE DONE WHAT WAS
OUR DUTY TO DO SO

Luke 17:10 says, "…We have done what was our duty to do so." In this context, the duty Jesus is referring to is to forgive. It is to declare to the Lord, "Lord, I forgive them." When you get an opportunity to speak with them, you declare to them, "I forgive you." Therefore it is settled in heaven and on earth. You must understand forgiveness is a faith matter and not a feeling matter. The subject of Jesus's discourse here is "forgiveness." Jesus has pointed out here that "Forgiveness is a faith walk." The Holy Spirit has shown us that the disciples' responsibility is to forgive. To forgive is my responsibility which is the other side of the privilege I have. I have the privilege of having the name of Jesus. I have the privilege of having the blood of Jesus on my side. I have the privilege of being able to use the word of God. I have the privilege of being able to cast out devils. I have the privilege of binding in heaven and on earth. The other side of having privilege is having the responsibility to forgive. Your faith will finish the job if you don't let up. No person can keep you from getting what belongs to you.

People Who Are Self Seeking

People who are self seeking are people who are no longer trusting God. Worldly people are self-seekers because they don't have God to depend on. But as a believer,

I believe God will go around or bypass others to give me what I need, because He says in Psalm 84:11, "…. the LORD will give grace and glory; No good *thing* will He withhold From those who walk uprightly."

How You Know You Have Forgiven

You know you have forgiven when you see your offender and your feelings don't hurt anymore. You will be smiling at them. You will be raised in three days at the most from an offense, because the same power that raised Jesus from death lives in you. While speaking to His disciples as explained in Matthew 18:21–35, Jesus said that you are to forgive seventy times seven in a day and settle accounts with all your servants. In this new covenant God does not forgive when you forgive. You are already forgiven. The tormentors are bitter envy, strife, and confusion. Where these three are, they invite all kinds of torments (evil works). When you don't forgive, you open yourself to all kinds of tormentors. Even though you have been forgiven, if *you* don't forgive, you open yourself to the torments of strife (self seeking or selfishness), envy, confusion, and all evil works. When you take the stand of unforgiveness, you are no longer representing your master as He is. You cut yourself off from the flow of God's blessings. Your finances shut down. Your body gets sick. Your mind is tormented. You are not at peace with anybody. You start wondering, "Why isn't God blessing me?" It is our duty to forgive and to guard against strife, envy, confusion, and all evil.

The issue is not about the offender, but the offended. The trap is set for you. Forgiveness is something to be done by faith. We must understand that someone along the way will misunderstand what we do or misinterpret something we say. Therefore, as Christians we must do everything in our power to communicate correct messages and bring healing and restoration whenever misunderstanding and offense occurs between ourselves and someone else.

When you catch yourself being a source of offense to someone else, it is important to take the mature path and ask that person to forgive you. Don't get defensive, because that will make the problem worse. It may even lead to a deeper conflict, so say you are sorry, ask for forgiveness, and move on!

Seek the wisdom of God, the power of the Holy Spirit. Use the word of God to overcome offense and destroy what the devil is trying to do between you and the other person. Make it your priority and personal objective or duty to help that other person overcome what he thinks you did or said. Sometimes it is more important to help the other person attain a position of peace than it is to prove who is right or wrong!

Romans 12:18 says, "If it be possible, as much as lieth in you, live peaceably with all men." In other words, If possible, as far as it depends on you, live at peace with everyone."

Hebrews 12:14 also says, "Follow peace with all men, and holiness, without which no man shall see the Lord." That is to say, strive to live in peace with everybody, and pursue that consecration and holiness without which no one will ever see the Lord.

6

THE SOURCE OF STRIFE

Everyone has an opportunity to get offended. Jesus said in Luke 17:1, "It is impossible but that offences will come." The word "impossible" comes from the Greek word *anendektos*, meaning something that is impossible, inadmissible, unallowable, or unthinkable. It is simply unthinkable that you would allow yourself to dream that you could live this life without an opportunity to become offended.

The Source of Strife

First of all, let us define the term strife so we can understand what we are addressing. Strife comes from the Greek word *eritheía,* meaning carnal ambition, selfish rivalry, self-seeking, acting for one's own gain regardless of the discord it causes, selfish ambition, and placing self-interest ahead of what the Lord declares right or good for others. It is discord or quarrel that can't be stopped once it gets going. It is the word for endless arguments and bitterness. God hates this behavior!

In a strife situation, both sides contribute to the tension. Arrogance on one side results in treachery on the other or harming someone who trusts you. Nobody wins, and things only get worse. The strife is not the intended state of existence. God created a world of harmony and intends His children to be peacemakers. Jesus left us with peace of heart and mind that is beyond understanding. Philippians 4:7 says, "And the peace of God, which passeth all understanding, shall keep your hearts and minds through Christ Jesus."

But how many of us still act as though we are living with Joseph and his eleven brothers? God hates strife because it is totally opposed to His reign of peace. Whether strife is dormant or active in your life, the weed is always going to be there until you dig it out and offer it to God. It is a sacrifice that needs to be burned up.

James 3:13–14 says, [13]Who is wise and understanding among you? Let him show by good conduct that his works are done in the meekness of wisdom. But if you have bitter envy and self-seeking (strife) in your hearts, do not boast and lie against the truth.

Sometimes you may be the offended one or the offender. Strife and offense are very serious matters because they negatively affects the move of God in the offended and the offender. Wisdom in scripture can be favorable or unfavorable. Wisdom can come from above or beneath. Wisdom is deeper than knowledge.

This Wisdom Does Not Descend from Above

A wisdom that does not come from above is earthly, sensual, and demonic. James 3:15 states, *15*This wisdom does not descend from above, but is earthly, sensual, demonic."

The wisdom referred to here is strife and envy. Strife and envy are earthy, sensual, and demonic. When one is in this realm, he is not in faith but in the sensory realm. One of the reasons the Bible cautions us about strife and bitter envy is because it takes us out of the spirit realm and into the sensory realm. The word *sensual* here does not mean erotic fantasy, feeling of sexual desire, or pleasure. It means it is part of the earthly wisdom that comes from the senses. The wisdom that does not come from above comes from the senses. The earthly wisdom is not born of the Spirit; it comes from another source other than God. In 1 Corinthians 14:33, Paul qualifies this statement: "[33] For God is not the author of confusion, but of peace, as in all the churches of the saints."

In Genesis 3:6, we see the tragedy of functioning in the sensory realm. "And when the woman saw that the tree was good for food, and that it was pleasant to the eyes, and a tree to be desired to make one wise, she took of the fruit thereof, and did eat, and gave also unto her husband with her; and he did eat." The desire to become wise seemed reasonable to the woman. Her definition of wise was human self-rule and not God dependency, as taught in Proverbs 1:7. "⁷The fear of the LORD *is* the beginning of knowledge, *But* fools despise wisdom and instruction."

Paul tells us in Galatians 5:16, "Walk in the Spirit, and you shall not fulfill the lust of the flesh." If you have bitter envy and self-seeking (strife) in your heart, that does not come from the Spirit of God. It comes from the senses. That means you are ruled and controlled by the senses.

Distraction Triplets

Where envy and strife exist, confusion and all evil things are there. James 3:16 states, "For where envying and strife is, there is confusion and every evil work." Envy and strife invite confusion and all kinds of evil and demonic activity. Envy, strife, and confusion are distraction triplets. Where envy is there, are strife and confusion. Where there is Strife there are Envy and Confusion. Where there is Confusion there are Strife and Envy. These three accompany one another. Wherever one is, the other two are close behind. They open dysfunction and frustration to a person's relationships, family, business, and ministry. Where ever there is Strife, Envy, and Confusion set a stage for demonic invasion. That is why the scripture cautions us about these distractions.

Where people are envious of others due to their position, access, proximity, or placement, there will be confusion and every evil work. Where people are envious and seeking for their own aggrandizement, visibility, fame, and fortune, there will be confusion and every evil work. The King James Bible version of James 3:16

puts it this way: "For where envying and strife is, there is confusion and every evil work."

Therefore, self-seeking is strife. Abraham's and Lot's servants were self-seeking. They were seeking for themselves. When we eliminate these traits from among ourselves, we begin to take dominion, control and rule. When we eliminate these from among ourselves, we get into agreement and become productive, fruitful, and multiplied. When we don't take offense and eliminate envy, strife, and confusion from among ourselves, we shall have done all those things that are commanded of us, and we will have done that which was our duty to do.

Wisdom That Is From Above

James 3:17 says, [17]But the wisdom that is from above is first pure, then peaceable, gentle, willing to yield, full of mercy and good fruits, without partiality and without hypocrisy." Many Christians want peace, but they don't have purity. People who don't have peace around themselves can't minister peace to others because they are impure. When you deal with a person who creates confusion and strife, you are dealing with someone who is impure. Their motive is not pure.

James 3:18 says, "Now the fruit of righteousness is sown in peace by those who make peace."

Envy, strife, and confusion open door to all kinds of evil activity. They open door to all kinds of evil activity that debilitate or weaken and that are dysfunctional in the anointing. What stops miracles from anointing is strife and the stuff that we come up with—strife in the leadership, strife among the brethren, strife in relationships.

The Number One Assault the Enemy Releases

Strife is the number one assault the enemy releases against a miracle ministry and the people of destiny. He is the author of confusion. 1 Corinthians 14:33 states, "For God is not the author of confusion, but of peace, as in all churches of the saints." He sends strife so he can confuse people of destiny with all kinds of evil to sop the moves of God. If strife continues among the believers the anointing will lift. The anointing will lift in relationships as well. Anointing will not function in an environment of strife, envy, and confusion. If we are going to move in the supernatural, we must understand that strife is our chief enemy.

7

THE SOURCE OF WARS AND FIGHTS

James 4:1–3 says, "Where do wars and fights come from among you? Do they not come from your desires for pleasure that war in your members? You lust and do not have. You murder and covet and cannot obtain. You fight and war. Yet you do not have because you do not ask. You ask and do not receive, because you ask amiss, that you may spend it on your pleasures."

Strife originates from three sources: desire for pleasure, internal wars, and lust of the flesh or jealousy. Wars and fights come from the desire for pleasure or lust that war in your members. James 4:2 says, "You lust and do not have. You murder and covet and cannot obtain. You fight and war. Yet you do not have because you do not ask." The word lust means a fleshly appetite that is attempting to be satisfied by fleshly means.

The scripture cautions us in Romans 13:13 to "walk properly, as in the day, not in revelry (merrymaking) and drunkenness, not in lewdness and lust, not in strife and envy." The word of God in Galatians 5:15–16 states, "15But if you bite and devour one another, take heed that you be not consumed one of another. 16This I say then, Walk in the Spirit, and ye shall not fulfil the lust of the flesh." It warns us to stop becoming sources of wars and fights, because if we bite and devour one another, we will consume one another!

We must stop becoming sources of wars and fights by walking in the Spirit. When you walk in the Spirit, you shall not fulfill the lust of the flesh. In other words, we stop becoming sources of wars and fights by getting a revelation of where they come from.

Ephesians 1:17 says "That the God of our Lord Jesus Christ, the Father of glory, may give to you the spirit of wisdom and revelation in the knowledge of Him." We stop becoming sources of wars and fights by getting the wisdom of the Holy Spirit. In Daniel 5:11, the scripture referencing Daniel says, "There is a man in your kingdom in whom is the Spirit of the Holy God. And in the days of your father, light and understanding and wisdom, like the wisdom of the gods, were found in him"

We stop becoming sources of wars and fights by transformation by the renewing of our minds to the Word of God. Romans 12:2 says, "And do not be conformed to this world, but be transformed by the renewing of your mind, that you may prove what is that good and acceptable and perfect will of God."

We stop from becoming sources of wars and fights by looking closely at ourselves to see whether we could be the source. 2 Corinthians 3:18 states, "But we all, with unveiled face, beholding as in a mirror the glory of the Lord, are being transformed into the same image from glory to glory, just as by the Spirit of the Lord."

The origin of wars and fights is the Soul.

The dictionary definition of soul is "an immaterial force within a human being thought to give the body life, energy, and power." Well, that's kind of ambiguous, (equivocal, nebulous, difficult to understand, and confusing. It is vague and not clearly defined. The revelation from the word of God is that the soul of a man is a component of the mind, the will, the emotions, and the attitudes. Therefore the origin of wars and fights is the soul. "What is among you" are wars and fights, and they are coming from what is within you, the soul, the outward man.

There is something in you that is causing wars and fights among you. We can manage what is manifesting among us by the revelation of what is within us. The strife, envy, wars, fights contentions, and divisions are an outward manifestation of something in you that is not in check. (The strife, envy, wars, fights, contentions, and divisions, are an outward manifestation of something in you that) is not under control. The strife, envy, wars, fights, contentions, and divisions, are an outward manifestation of something in you into which the Holy Spirit has not been allowed to move into. The strife, envy, wars, fights, contentions, and divisions, are an outward manifestation of something in you that you have not acknowledged that is in you. You have not acknowledged that there is something within you that is causing wars and fights—either because you are afraid of acknowledging it before God, or you are afraid of rejection of Him.

The fact of the matter is that God has accepted you because of what is inside you. What is inside you cannot change without Him. God's loving kindness drew you to Him because you could not be transformed without Him. You should never be ashamed to admit before God what is inside you. Any person who cannot acknowledge issues to you cannot acknowledge them before God either. Anybody who is always dealing with the same issue has not been honest with God relative to the issue and will not be honest with you either. Matthew and Luke in the gospels and the first letter of John lets us know that our souls are at war with what is in the world.

Matthew 16:26 says, "For what profit is it to a man if he gains the whole world, and loses his own soul? Or what will a man give in exchange for his soul?" The statement in this verse is self-evident in the sphere of the lower life. It does not profit from anything to gain the whole world if you lose your life because you cannot enjoy your possession. A life lost cannot be recovered at any price. Jesus wishes His disciples to understand that the soul, the spiritual life, is incommensurable with any outward possession, however great, and if it is forfeited, the loss is irrevocable. This theme is Christ's doctrine of the absolute worth of man as a moral subject. The man who grasps it will find it easy to be a hero and face any experience. To Jesus Christ, it is a self-evident truth.

Apostle Luke presents it a little differently from Matthew. In Luke 9:25, he says, "For what profit is it to a man if he gains the whole world, and is himself destroyed or lost?"

According to the above quoted scripture, all worldly things are worthless when compared to the life of the body. In the same respect, worldly things are worthless when compared to the soul and its state of never-ending enjoyment. People lose their souls for the unprofitable indulgence from mere disregard and forsaking Christ, who is the price at which Satan buys their souls. Yet one soul is worth more than all the world. Christ knows the price of souls because he redeemed them. He would not underrate the world because he made it. Let us then learn rightly to value our souls, acknowledging Christ is the only savior of them.

1 John 2:16 says, "For all that is in the world—the lust of the flesh, the lust of the eyes, and the pride of life—is not of the Father but is of the world." We may desire and possess worldly goods, and we can use them for the purpose for which God intended. We are to use them by his grace and to his glory. Born-again believers must not seek or value them for those purposes to which sin abuses them. The world draws the heart from God, and the more the love of the world prevails, the more the love of God decays. The things of the world are categorized according to the three ruling affections of corrupt nature.

1.   The lust of the flesh is the same as lust of the body. It means the wrong desires

of the heart and the appetite of indulging all things that excite and inflame sensual pleasures.

2.	The lust of the eyes means the eyes are delighted with riches and possessions. Having a craving for possession is the lust of covetousness. It is showing a very strong desire for something that you do not have, especially for something that belongs to someone else.

3.	The pride of life is a feeling that you are more important or better than other people. It is proud or disdainful behavior or treatment, as well as the splendor of a vainglorious life. The things of the world quickly fade and die away.

In 1 Corinthians 7:31 it states, "Those who use the things of the world, as if not engrossed in them. For this world in its present form is passing away." In 1 John

2:17, it says, "The world and its desires pass away, but whoever does the will of God lives forever."

Desire itself will before long, fail and cease, but holy affection is not like the lust that passes away. The love of God shall never fail.

1 John 2:16 says, "[16]For everything in the world—the lust of the flesh, the lust of the eyes, and the pride of life—comes not from the Father but from the world."

The meaning of 1 John 2:16 cannot easily be misunderstood. This victory over the world begins by faith in God, and a man has no root in him- or herself. He or she will fall away or at most remain an unfruitful contestant.

1 John 5:4 states, "For everyone born of God overcomes the world. This is the victory that has overcome the world, even

our faith." These vanities are so alluring to the corruption in our hearts that without constant watching and prayer, we cannot escape the world or obtain victory over the god and prince of it. If there is no profit in trade-off of the soul and the lower life for the whole world, how much less is there in exchanging the higher? When that forfeiture has been incurred, what price can he then pay to buy it back? None. "It costs more to redeem their souls, so that he must let that alone forever"

8

DEALING WITH CULPRITS OF WARS AND FIGHTS

God says your ability to change people who cannot be honest with God concerning destructive, devastating, disastrous, ruinous issues is ineffectual or counterproductive. Don't get into a fight with them; don't get into strife with them. They have not allowed the Holy Spirit to change them. They have never acknowledged the need for God to change them. Your effort to change people who have never acknowledged the need for God to change them is counterproductive.

Your best bet is to get away from them, lest they drive demonic activity into you.

Desire for Pleasure

The first origin of strife is the soul's desire for pleasure. Strife comes from lusting for something that will give you pleasure. It comes from something you want that will please you when you get or do it. Strife, wars, and fights come because there is something you want that will give you sensual gratification when you do get it. You get into strife with people because of something they did or got from you, or you are in strife with them because of something you want from them. You can hardly get into strife if you don't want anything. Jesus, your Lord, did not get into strife with those who crucified Him because He did not want anything from them. He wanted to give them something. He released forgiveness to them and forgave them undeservedly. There is nothing He wanted from them that would please Him. Jesus was here to please the Father; He did not need to win here on earth. Strife comes from the need to win. Born-again believers are sons in the kingdom of their Father. They have the character, nature, and authority of their Father and Lord Jesus the Christ.

The scripture in 1 John 3:2 tells us who we are. "Beloved, now are we the sons of God, and it doth not yet appear what we shall be: but we know that, when he shall appear, we shall be like Him; for we shall see Him as He is." Born again believers are here to please the Father. We don't want to win anything that will give you sensual gratification when you do get it. Like the Lord Jesus, we don't need to win here on earth because we now know strife comes from the soul's need to win.

Internal Wars

The second origin of strife is internal wars within your soul. Galatians 5:17 says, "For the flesh lusts against the Spirit, and the Spirit against the flesh; and these are contrary to one another, so that you do not do the things that you wish."

An internal war is that which is unexpressed, unexamined, and undealt with. The external wars you have among you, are manifestations of the internal war within you that you have not expressed, examined, and dealt with. Attempting to win an external war without would be inconsequential or trivial exercise without winning the war within. It would be in vain attempting to win with only your own ingenuity. You are able to win only with God's help. He is able to handle any situation you bring to Him. Jeremiah 32:27 says, "Behold, I am the Lord, the

God of all flesh. Is there anything too hard for Me? There is nothing too hard for The Lord."

Asking Is a Requirement of the Human Soul

The war within you is because of something you have not asked the Father for. James 4:2–3 says, "Ye lust, and have not: ye kill, and desire to have, and cannot obtain: ye fight and war, yet ye have not, because ye ask not. Ye ask, and receive not, because ye ask amiss, that ye may consume it upon your lusts." Ask God what you are not getting, and He will handle it for you.

Your Father in heaven tells you in John 15:7, "If you abide in Me, and My words abide in you, you will ask what you desire, and it shall be done for you." You get into strife because you ask from people who don't have what you need. What you need is with the Father. Tell the Father, give me the love I am missing, satisfaction I am missing, self-esteem I am missing, comfort I am missing, recognition I am missing, peace I am missing, joy I am missing, kindness I am missing." Only the Father can give you all these invisible attributes.

Romans 1:20 says, "For since the creation of the world His invisible attributes are clearly seen, being understood by the things that are made, even His eternal power and Godhead, so that they are without excuse." Other relationships cannot give you what you need. You need to ask the Father by faith for whatever you need and He will give it to you. It can come only from the Father. Asking is a requirement of the human soul to receive everything you ask. The reason you don't have something is because you haven't asked by faith. You ask a miss because you use your senses to ask from people who walk by the senses. You get into strife because you are attempting to get what you want by the sight senses. You are supposed to walk by faith. You ask a miss because you are asking for your pleasure. You are not asking for God's purpose. Your objective is pleasure, not God's kingdom. The million-dollar question is, "When you feel better about yourself, what will you do for the kingdom of God?"

Jealousy or Lust

The third origin of strife from our text in James 4:1–3 is jealousy within your soul. 1 Corinthians 3:3 says, "For you are still of the flesh. For while there is jealousy and strife among you, are you not of the flesh and behaving only in a human way?" The definition of jealousy is bitter envy, fervency of mind, unfavorable sense, and feeling angry or unhappy because you wish you had what somebody else has. It's wanting to keep or protect something because it makes you feel proud.

Jealousy is the key source of strife (wars and fights). A person who is perpetually manifesting strife has serious issues of jealous. James 3:14 says, "[14]But if you have bitter envy and self-seeking in your hearts, do not boast and lie against the truth." 1 John 2:15–17 states, "[15] Do not love the world or the things in the world. If anyone loves the world, the love of the Father is not in him. [16]For all that is in the world—the lust of the flesh, the lust of the eyes, and the pride of life—is not of the Father but is of the world. And the world is passing away, and the lust of it; but he who does the will of God abides forever."

Do not set your affection or live sacrificially on behalf of anything that appeals to your fleshly appetite. Do not set your affection or live sacrificially on behalf of anything that appeals to your covetousness, or your greed. Do not set your affection or live sacrificially on behalf of anything that fosters pride or arrogance. Do not allow anything to lessen even slightly your worship, service, and devotion to God.

First Corinthians 3:1–3 says, "And I, brethren, could not speak to you as to spiritual people but as to carnal, as to babes in Christ. ² I fed you with milk and not with solid food; for until now you were not able to receive it, and even now you are still not able; ³for you are still carnal. For where there are envy, strife, and divisions among you, are you not carnal and behaving like mere men?"

"And I, brethren, could not speak unto you"

Apostle Paul was a spiritual man. He had spiritual gifts, including the extraordinary gifts of the Spirit. He could judge all things and had the mind of Christ. He was able to speak the wisdom of God in a mystery, yet he could not speak it to them because they were carnal and behaving like mere men. We must grow to spiritual maturity for the Spirit of God to speak spiritual things to us. God is not going to give what belongs to His mature children to babies because they will not know how to properly appropriate it. They will misappropriate it and risk destruction because they do not have spiritual discernment. Hosea 4:6 says, "My people are destroyed for lack of knowledge. Because you have rejected knowledge, I also will reject you from being priest for Me; Because you have forgotten the law of your God, I also will forget your children." Born-again believers are priests according to 1 Peter 2:9. "But you are a chosen generation, a royal priesthood, a holy nation, His own special people, that you may proclaim the praises of Him who called you out of darkness into His marvelous light."

"As to spiritual"

All of us are born of the Spirit of God. The Corinthian believers had the Spirit of God in them, as well as a work of grace upon them. They were the temple of God, and God's Spirit dwelt in them. They were washed, sanctified, and justified in the name of the Lord Jesus and by the Spirit of our God, but they did not have spiritual discerning or judgment in spiritual things. They were under great spiritual deterioration and did not have those spiritual frames or that spiritual experience and conversation. Similarly, when believers fail to grow to spiritual maturity, they remain carnal and as babes in Christ. The consequences of this spiritual retardation are envy, strife, and divisions among themselves.

"But as unto carnal"

The carnal state of the Corinthians believers at this time that the apostle is referencing is not as unregenerate men, but those who had carnal conceptions of things, were in carnal frames of soul, and walked into a carnal conversation with each other. Although they were not in the flesh, in a state of nature, the flesh was in them and not only lusted against the Spirit but was very predominant in them. It held them captive so that they were dominated by it. Most believers are in this state of affairs, and yet they expect the Spirit of God to send them spiritual things.

"Even as unto babes in Christ"

These Corinthians' believers were in Christ and so were new creatures. They were in the faith of Christ, though they were babes and wimps or ineffectual. They were believers in Christ, converted persons yet they were children in understanding, knowledge, and experience. They had but little judgment in spiritual things and were ineffective in the word of righteousness. This is the case with most born-again believers today, though others were enriched in all utterance and knowledge, and in no gift do they come behind their fellow spiritual born-again believers.

1 Corinthians 3:3 says "envying," which means jealousy and rivalry and refers to

feelings of the immature, born-again Christians. "Strife" refers to their words, and "divisions" refers to their actions. It is evident that envying produces strife, and strife creates divisions (factious parties). Galatians 5:19–21 lists the work of the flesh, which manifests in the life of immature Christian. "[9]Now the works of the flesh are evident, which are: adultery, fornication, uncleanness, lewdness, [20]idolatry, sorcery, hatred, contentions, jealousies, outbursts of wrath, selfish ambitions, dissensions, heresies, [21] envy, murders, drunkenness, revelries, and the like; of which I tell you beforehand, just as I also told you in time past, that those who practice such things will not inherit the kingdom of God." The word *carnal* (life on earth, especially as opposed to that in heaven) is used for *"strife"* which is a "work of the flesh." The "flesh" includes all feelings that aim not at the glory of

God and the good of our neighbor, but at gratifying the self.

Galatians 5:22–23 records the manifestations of mature or spiritual born again believers. "[22]But the fruit of the Spirit is love, joy, peace, longsuffering, kindness, goodness, faithfulness, [23] gentleness, self-control. Against such there is no law." Those mature or spiritual born-again believers are in the upper class of Christ. They have crucified the flesh with its passions and desires. They walk by faith, not by the senses. If we live in the Spirit, let us also walk in the Spirit. Let us not become conceited, provoking one another and envying one another like immature or unspiritual believers who walk by sensory not by faith. They are of a lower class.

1 Corinthians 3:3 says, "For you are still carnal. For where there are envy, strife,

and divisions among you, are you not carnal and behaving like mere men? To be carnally minded is a death sentence.

Romans 8:6 states, "⁶For to be carnally minded is death, but to be spiritually minded is life and peace."

"For to be carnally minded is death"

The carnal mind includes the largest part of a corrupt person. That is the mind, the understanding, the judgment, the will, the affections, the thoughts, and the reasonings of a person. It may be translated as "the wisdom" or the "prudence of the flesh," to distinguish it from wisdom, which is from above. Carnal is that natural and civil wisdom that is applaudable or commendable and shows the wisest part of man. Everyone destitute of the grace of God is anxious herein. This is applicable to all the sensualist, the worldling, the proud, the hypocritical, censoriousthe self-righteous, and the opposers of this world. This wisdom of the flesh, or carnal mindedness, "is death" because it is separation from God. It is the end of carnal mindedness. When carnal mindedness prevails in the saints, it brings a death upon them. Sometimes they are very dead and lifeless in their frames, in the exercise of grace and discharge of duty. The lifelessness situation in their frames, in the exercise of grace, and in the discharge of duty is their carnality. Since it alienates them from God, renders them transgressors of God's law, and makes unpleasant in a way that people feel offended, annoyed, or disgusted. It sets the soul against and diverts it from Christ's way of life. If grace does not prevent it, it will cause eternal separation from God. Carnality is sin and sinful; it is enmity with God. It disqualifies one for life and makes persons fit companions for the heirs of wrath.

"But to be spiritually minded, is life and peace"

The only living people in a spiritual sense are spiritually minded Christians. Everything of and after the flesh causes spiritual death. So far as carnal mindedness prevails in those who profess it, there is a deadness in them as it pertains to spiritual exercises. When it comes to outward appearance, there is no difference between them and dead men. Spiritually minded men are evidently the living people. They have a spiritual discerning of spiritual things; They breathe after them, savor and relish them. They talk of spiritual things, and walk in a spiritual manner. The spiritual born-again believers are not only alive but lively in the exercise of grace and the discharge of duty. They are the means of energizing others. Their end will be everlasting life or unstoppable life, which is certain from the declared will and promise of God, and from the grace and Spirit of life that is in them.

"Peace"

1.   Peace is another effect of spiritual mindedness, and it's a delight to enjoy peace of conscience. This is a fruit of the Spirit; this is a part of the kingdom of grace. The things their minds are conversant with are products of the gift of God, which passes all understanding. It has more worth than the world. Such men are also of a peaceable nature in their relationships families, and churches. Their end will be absolute and eternal peace.

9

THE PRACTICE OF FORGIVENESS

A neighbor is literally the one who is in our proximity. It is the one who is near to us by acts of kindness and friendship or relationship. Our relationships contain many people with the potential to hurt us, very often in small, ongoing ways. These relationships include but are not limited to husband, wife, son, daughter, brother, sister, mother, father, friends, colleagues, and neighbors. We dismiss these hurts by trying to be good people. We think we are not vindictive, retaliatory, or overly sensitive, believing these things shouldn't bother us. But they do. They affect us because our self-regard is like a magnet, and resentments are attracted to it.

What is the impact of holding onto these resentments? Jesus taught the art of forgiveness. "Lord, how many times shall I forgive my brother or sister who sins against me? Up to seven times?' Jesus answered, "Jesus said to him, "*I do not say to you, up to seven times, but up to seventy times seven*" Yes, and more. Matthew 18:21–22 states, [21] Then Peter came to Him and said, 'Lord, how often shall my brother sin against me, and I forgive him? Up to seven times?' [22] Jesus said to him, 'I do not say to you, up to seven times, but up to seventy times seven.' We are to forgive the culprit as often as he sins. Our forgiveness is to know no limits, that is, it is to be eternal and timeless, which is holy" Also, Matthew 5:42–46 says, "[44] But I say to you, love your enemies, bless those who curse you, do good to those who hate you, and pray for those who spitefully use you and persecute you [45]that you may be sons of your Father in heaven; for He makes His sun rise on the evil and on the good, and sends rain on the just and on the unjust."

God's word in Leviticus 19:18 commands us to love our neighbor. "[18] You shall not take vengeance, nor bear any grudge against the children of your people, but you shall love your neighbor as yourself: I am the LORD." Loving your neighbor and hating your enemy was generally believed or imagined to mean that if we loved the one, we must hate the other. In Romans 12:17–20, the scripture warns us, "Repay no one evil for evil. Have regard for good things in the sight of all men. If it is possible, as much as depends on you, live peaceably with all men. [19]Beloved, do not avenge yourselves, but rather give place to wrath;

for it is written, 'Vengeance is Mine, I will repay,' says the Lord. [20] Therefore 'If your enemy is hungry, feed him; If he is thirsty, give him a drink; For in so doing you will heap coals of fire on his head.'"

Love Your Enemies

"Loving your enemies" means loving them in God's way—unconditionally. The God kind of love is not a feeling or an emotion, as it has been erroneously taught and misconstrued by many, but a decision we make. It is God's command to love. Whenever God tells us to do something, He expects us to exercise our faith and do it regardless of whether we feel like doing it. God does everything by faith, and because we have God's image, we are to do everything the way God does it - by faith. You decide to love by faith. Actually, if you believe you can love, and you say you love, you end up loving that person, regardless of his transgression against you, because you love by applying faith. The feeling is a manifestation of loving, not the love itself. When you are persuaded you can actually love, you add your corresponding action of saying you love people, and the outcome is you love them. Therefore whether or not the feeling of loving them comes, your decision of loving them does not change.

At the cross of Calvary Jesus was not feeling all happy when He was undergoing the whipping, the tearing off his flesh, and the bleeding in agony. He cried in pain to the Father and said, "If there was possibly another way of redeeming mankind please do it, nevertheless not my will by yours." He finally made a faith decision to love man in his sinful nature, and the Father's will was done. The description of faith love is seen in 1 Corinthians 13:4–8.

"'⁴Love suffers long and is kind; love does not envy; love does not parade itself, is not puffed up; ⁵does not behave rudely, does not seek its own, is not provoked, thinks no evil; ⁶does not rejoice in iniquity, but rejoices in the truth; ⁷ bears all things, believes all things, hopes all things, endures all things. ⁸ Love never fails."

These inherent characteristics of love do not contain the feeling ingredient. They are corresponding actions to one's persuasion. We are to love people, but to disapprove of their unbecoming conduct. This is the love of benevolence of which Jesus approves, and we are to use it toward our enemies. It is humanly impossible to love the conduct of a person who curses and reviles us, who injures our person or property, or who violates all the laws of God. Although we may hate his conduct and suffer keenly when we are affected by it, yet we may still wish well to the person. We may pity his madness and folly. We may speak kindly of and to him, return good for evil, aid him in the time of his trial, pursue to do him good, and promote his eternal welfare hereafter.

Romans 12:17–20 says, "[17]Do not repay anyone evil for evil. Be careful to do what is right in the eyes of everyone. [18] If it is possible, as far as it depends on you, live at peace with everyone. [19]Do not take revenge, my dear friends, but leave room for God's wrath, for it is written: 'It is mine to avenge; I will repay, says the Lord. [20] On the contrary: 'If your enemy is hungry, feed him; if he is thirsty, give him something to drink. In doing this, you will heap burning coals on his head." This is what is meant by loving our enemies. It is a special law of Christianity and is the highest possible test of devotion to God. It's probably the most difficult of all duties to be performed by human effort. It is a work of grace.

"That you may be sons of your Father in heaven." Your heavenly Father is ever forgiving. You are to be forgiving like your Father. You have His image, character, nature, and authority. You resemble Him. You are like your Father in heaven when you do on earth what He does in or from heaven. The Lord Jesus teaches that we must do real kindness to all, especially to their souls. We must pray for them. Many will render good for good, but we must render good for evil; this will speak a nobler principle than most men. Others salute their brethren and embrace those of their own ways and opinions, but we must not so confine our respect. It is the duty of Christians to desire, aim at, and press toward perfection in grace and holiness, and therein we must study to conform ourselves to the example of our heavenly Father.

Promise Of Forgiveness

The Lord promises that forgiveness is possible even when hurt seems too great to bear and repair. God promises to remove a heart of stone and give a heart of flesh to those who heed His word. Ezekiel 11:19 says, "I will remove from them their heart of stone and give them a heart of flesh." A heart of stone is unforgiveness and is experienced when we are too angry, too selfish, or too frozen by the pain others have caused us.

Although a heart of flesh may be susceptible or easily hurt, harmed physically, mentally, or emotionally, it is benevolent and compassionate. A heart of flesh sees that while we are feeling pain, the other person may also be hurting for the pain he caused us. We are to be careful not to be so caught up in ourselves that we do not notice another is struggling from the offense. Of course people need to be held accountable for their actions, but these people also need patience from us, just as the servant said to his master, "Be patient with me." Matthew 18:26 states, "[26] The servant therefore fell down before him, saying, 'Master, have patience with me, and I will pay you all.'"

When we are practicing patience with others, holding onto the hope and vision for our relationship with them is a true act of benevolence or compassion. We need to invite the Lord into the journey and ask for the courage it takes for us to be patient with one another, and for the understanding needed to see that they are also working through the pain that needs forgiveness.

10

RESENTMENTS AND A
FAULTY WORLDVIEW

Sometimes we shy away from forgiveness because of the idea that forgiveness means sins are washed away. We sometimes think that forgiveness means forgetting, and that feels wrong. Sometimes we feel that resentments educate us about the people in the world around us and guide us in the ways we should act toward them. We feel like the memories of our past hurts help us maintain boundaries with people. But the Lord is all-knowing and is mercy itself. Therefore, there must be a way for knowing and forgiveness to exist together, a clearheaded forgiveness that forgets nothing and forgives all. You know you have forgiven when you can look at someone who has hurt you and not feel anger. Yes, this is possible. Those who have charity hardly notice the evil in another person; instead, they notice all the good and truths that are his. They place a good interpretation on his evils and falsities. This is God's nature and of such a nature are all those who function like God does, by faith. Followers have this nature from the Lord, who bends everything evil into good. Now, this doesn't negate the fact that we need to protect ourselves from people who make a habit of hurting us. The key is to invite the Lord into the process. It is the Lord who will keep us separated from our resentments, if we let Him. We must be strict, tough, and disciplined in our endeavors to forgive. Love must be tough. We must get used to naming each hurt and resentment by speaking to them the word of God, the way the Godhead speaks to them. God's and the Bible's faith empowers us to do this. We must do it seventy times seven times, which means all the time, every time any time, and without limit.

The Power of Forgiveness

When we forgive others, there is a freedom, the grace where we are no longer shackled by our own anger. It moves us from our selfish senses to knowing the truth. John 8:32 says, "And you shall know the truth, and the truth shall make you free." But letting go of the fantasies that we can change the past, that we can change others, or even that we are the ones who can change ourselves opens room for God to help us safeguard the resentment we feel. Each time we forgive, it paves the way for the next time we need to forgive. Practicing God's way of doing things using courage and patience, and letting the Lord into the process of forgiveness, is like exercising a muscle: it grows stronger and stronger. We grow from glory to glory, from goodness to goodness. 2 Corinthians 3:18 says, "But we all, with unveiled face, beholding as in a mirror the glory of the Lord, are being transformed into the same image from glory to glory, just as by the Spirit of the Lord."

By God's grace, we can come to a point where forgiveness is intuitive. By God's grace we can come to a point where forgiveness is having the ability to know or understand things without any proof or evidence. By God's grace, we can come to a point where forgiveness is a blessed way to live.

11

TAMING THE TONGUE

No person can tame the tongue, but that does not mean the tongue cannot be tamed. The tongue can be tamed by the word of God. The scripture in James 3:2–13 tells us the process by which the tongue is tamed.

> "²For we all stumble in many things. If anyone does not stumble in word, he is a perfect man, able also to bridle the whole body. ³Indeed, we put bits in horses' mouths that they may obey us, and we turn their whole body. ⁴Look also at ships: although they are so large and are driven by fierce winds,

they are turned by a very small rudder wherever the pilot desires. [5]Even so the tongue is a little member and boasts great things. See how great a forest a little fire kindles! [6]And the tongue is a fire, a world of iniquity. The tongue is so set among our members that it defiles the whole body, and sets on fire the course of nature; and it is set on fire by hell. [7]For every kind of beast and bird, of reptile and creature of the sea, is tamed and has been tamed by mankind. [8]But no man can tame the tongue. It is an unruly evil, full of deadly poison. [9]With it we bless our God and Father, and with it we curse men, who have been made in the similitude of God. [10]Out of the same mouth proceed blessing and cursing. My brethren, these things ought not to be so. [11]Does a spring send forth fresh water and bitter from the same opening? Can a fig

> tree, my brethren, bear olives, or a grapevine bear figs? Thus no spring yields both salt water and fresh. [13]Who is wise and understanding among you? Let him show by good conduct that his works are done in the meekness of wisdom."

The tongue is the instrument Satan uses to cause strife in relationships that are destined to accomplish the purposes of God on earth. The way God accomplishes His purpose is through the anointing. Anointing is a symbolic of blessing, protection, and empowerment. To anoint means to consecrate for office or God's service, and the meaning of the word "anointed" is "chosen one."

God does not lift the anointing, the blessing, the protection, and the empowerment. Neither does He stop His move. He anoints people for a specific purpose in furthering His kingdom. As

1 John 2:20 says, "[20] But you have an anointing from the Holy One, and you know all things."

The anointing is not temporary but is eternal. The anointing outlives the anointed. We see a perfect example with Elisha: long after he died, the anointing was still at work, resurrecting dead people.

Second Kings 13:21 says, "And they put the man in the tomb of Elisha; and when the man was let down and touched the bones of Elisha, he revived and stood on his feet." God has anointed us, and He has sealed and given us the Holy Spirit in our hearts as a guarantee. As 2 Corinthians 1:21–22 states, "Now He who establishes us with you in Christ and has anointed us is God, who also has sealed us and given us the Spirit in our hearts as a guarantee."

What lifts the anointing and stops God's move is strife. The weapon the enemy uses to destroy God's anointing and move is strife. Strife manifests because something is missing in people's lives. In the matter of offense between believers, right or wrong is immaterial at this point. Who is right and who is wrong becomes immaterial. Right or wrong is not the issue—peace is the issue. Strife and contention can only be perpetuated when someone has to win. If you won't let go, then it means you have to win; it means you are more interested in winning than in peace. The fruit of righteousness is sown in peace by those who seek and make peace. We must always be in pursuit of peace with all men.

James 3:18 says, "Now the fruit of righteousness is sown in peace by those who make peace." Born-again believers pursue the things *which make* for peace and the things by which one may edify another. By doing so, there will be no interest in winning. They seek peace. James 3:2–13 teaches that the tool of strife is the tongue. One small spark can burn down a whole forest. Similarly, if the tongue is not checked, it will bring down a whole house, relationship, marriage, business, and a ministry organization. The tongue is fire, a world of iniquity. The Bible makes a comparison of small sparks and a forest, a big horse and a small bit, a big ship and a small rudder, and a big situation and a small tongue. That means in the same way a small spark has the ability to burn a whole forest, a bit can turn a big horse, and a rudder can turn a whole ship, the tongue - given the opportunity will turn a situation, ministry organization, business organization, household, relationship, family, or marriage. The tongue has the ability to turn a situation, ministry organization, business organization, household, relationship, family, or marriage around for the worse through strife, or for the better through God's word. Someone will probably say, "oh! I need the power of God in my situation; ministry organization, household, relationship, family, or marriage. No! you don't need the power of God in my situation. May I submit to you that you have the power to tame the tongue. Proverbs 18:21 tells us that death and life are in power of the tongue. Another person may say, oh! "I want the Lord in the situation." No! The Lord is in the situation because He is in you.

John 14:23 says, "²³Jesus answered and said to him, If anyone loves Me, he will keep My word; and My Father will love him, and We will come to him and make Our home with him." All you need to do is to tame your tongue. You need your tongue to be silent. The Bitter envy and strife are perpetuated by the tongue. The tongue is so set among our members that it destroys the whole body. The tongue sets on fire the course of nature, and it is set on fire by hell because that was our nature before we were born again. Out of the same mouth proceeds blessing and cursing. The tongue is set among our members such that it heals the whole body. Proverb 12:18 states, "There is one who speaks like the piercings of a sword, But the tongue of the wise promotes health."

Matthew 12:34–36 says, "How can you, being evil, speak good things? For out of the abundance of the heart the mouth speaks. [35] A good man out of the good treasure of his heart brings forth good things, and an evil man out of the evil treasure brings forth evil things. [36] But I say to you that for every idle word men may speak, they will give account of it in the day of judgment."

Technology

Technology has provided the Internet: Email, Text messaging, Facebook, YouTube, Twitter, WhatsApp, Instagram as a wonderful instrument of communication network. It is a powerful way of instantaneously communicating the gospel around the world. Unfortunately, many have abused it and use it to perpetuate all kinds of evil works. Are these now new tools meant to sin with? To the born-again believers, the Internet does not give us license to gossip and backbite. Some born-again believers are using this instrument to cause enmity, as if Jesus of Nazareth does not see it. He sees it with disdain. There is need for some discipline and restraint.

Proverbs 15:3 says, "The eyes of the Lord are in every place, beholding the evil and the good." When we use e-mail, text messages, Facebook, YouTube, Twitter, WhatsApp, and Instagram to sin, it is equivalent to saying and doing it. There is no difference. When you stop gossip, strife ceases.

TALEBEARER OR
PIECE ROLLER

The scripture in Proverbs 26:20 declares, "Where no wood is, there the fire goes out: so where there is no talebearer, the strife ceases." The scripture does not have the word *gossip*, but uses the word T*alebearer*. The word *talebearer* in Hebrew means Nirgan, Roller of pieces, betrayer, gossipmonger, and newsmonger. It means one that spreads gossips or rumors, who habitually reveals personal or sensational facts about others. Talebearer is the biblical equivalent of gossip: it's one who provides information about another's wrongdoings.

A roller of pieces or talebearer will tear you in pieces and will only tell you half the truth. Where there is no wood, the fire goes out. Where there is no talebearer or gossiper, strife ceases: yes strife stops. Where there is nobody using his tongue to eternalize gossip, strife stops. Strife and contention cannot be immortalized without somebody speaking them into existence. The most spiritual and loving thing to do in a strife situation is to be quiet and turn away. That is not rude—it stops immortalizing the contention. The most spiritual and loving thing to do during strife is to say, "I won't be a part of it," and walk away. Don't explain anything. Ignore them and do not participate. Get wise and get out of the strife.

A talebearer or roller of pieces will only roll to you a part of what he wants you to know. Anybody who is eternalizing or constantly causing strife and contention is a roller of pieces. People will not tell you everything, just the negative pieces of information they want you to know. The scripture declares that, the first person to speak is always right until his friend tells the other side. Proverbs 18:17 declares, "The first one to plead his cause seems right, Until his neighbor comes and examines him." Therefore do not judge anything until you have heard the other side.

1 3

TAKING A STAND AGAINST STRIFE

First recognize that strife is a trap against you. Do not hang out with talebearers. They look all happy and joyous when they are telling all these tales, but they don't have joy themselves, and they are not happy. Their lives are a mess. Their situations or conditions are very dirty, untidy, complicated, and difficult to deal with. They don't have peace. They seem to be okay, but so much is happening to them.

The tongue is the apparatus the enemy uses to cause strife. It is the instrument the enemy uses to cause discord among the people of destiny, in order to stop God's purpose. It is rolled to strife, but they roll it to God instead. If the rollers fail to roll it to God, Jesus; the Word will throw it back at them.

Proverbs 18:8 states, "[8]The words of a talebearer are like tasty trifles, And they go down into the inmost body."

There are people who are sick because of words spoken against them. There are people who are sick because of rolling pieces. There are people who are sick because of words rolled against them. There are people who are sick because they rolled pieces. There are people who are diseased and sick because they entertained words about people in their lives. These piece rollers get offended and angry, and they stop the rivers of living water from flowing. They are now dealing with addictions and with torments because they rolled pieces. They have been trapped because gossip gets into the inmost body.

If you get into strife regardless of how anointed, gifted, talented, or good you may be, you will constantly fall short of achieving or fulfilling God's purpose in your life. The distraction triplets will open a person, marriage, family, relationship, or ministry to dysfunction, confusion, and every evil work. Strife is the key enemy of disrupting the plans, purpose, and everything else you are engaged in doing for the kingdom of God. If strife is allowed to function or go unchecked, it will disrupt the plans of God. The scripture is clear: where bitter envy and strife exist, you are opening the door to every evil work.

Avoid Strife

The reason strife and envy manifest is because of an unrenewed mind, or a mind that is not being renewed to the word of God. The reason strife and envy manifest is because of a failure to think in line with the word of God. Therefore you and I are to guard ourselves against offense. We are to refuse to participate in strife. Second Timothy 2:23 gives us some insight as to how strife comes. If I know how strife comes, then I will have some insight how to overcome it. The scripture here instructs us to avoid foolish and ignorant disputes, knowing that they generate strife.

The word *foolish* means moron, which is a Hebrew word meaning "An offensive way of referring to somebody that you think to be very stupid. Lack of good judgment. To be dull. To be stupid as

in blockheaded. To be close minded."
The mind is blocked; nothing is getting
in. Being foolish doesn't mean lacking
intelligence.

Intelligence means the ability to learn,
understand, or think in a logical way
about things. Intelligence means the
ability to do things well. When you
deal with people who are blockheaded,
usually nothing you say penetrates their
minds. All they want to do is express their
opinions. That means they are no longer
in conversation or dialogue. The word
ignorant means uninstructed or unlearned.
Listen what God's word says: avoid it
(ignorant disputes). At this point, it is not
important that I am right and you are
wrong. What is important now is we be
at peace with each other.

In all relationships, especially in kingdom
relationships, when you deal with a child

of God, you are dealing with someone who has the blessing (empowerment to prosper) on him or her. When you curse or disregard someone with the blessing on him or her, you get the backside of that blessing, and both of you walk away with it.

The Bible tells us not to get into strife with anybody, but certainly not with someone in the household of faith. The reason is because now you are dealing with someone else with the blessing on them. God says in Genesis 12:3, "I will bless (empower to prosper) those who bless (empower to prosper) you, and I will curse (disregard) him who curses(disregard) you; And in you all the families of the earth shall be blessed (empowered to prosper)."

The word of God says in Proverbs 17:27–28, "²⁷ *He who has knowledge spares his words, and a man of understanding is of a calm spirit.*

*²⁸ Even a fool is counted wise when he holds his peace. When he shuts his lips, he is considered perceptive (*discerning, insightful).*"

Therefore whenever the discussion gets heated and the discourse becomes amplified, the man with knowledge spares his words. The person who is more peaceful in that engagement may not be the weak one or the one who is wrong. It is not about weakness or wrongdoing, but having discernment and avoiding discord, conflict, and strife. It is about making up for peace. In our culture today, it seems like the one who yells or speaks louder is the one who is right. Sometimes silence is the wisest thing you can speak. The man with calm spirit understands if the discussion continues, there is going to be strife.

Proverbs 14:7 says, "Go from the presence of a foolish man, when you do not perceive in him the lips of knowledge."

That means when you get a sense the other party is talking foolishness, dismiss yourself. You've got to stop being so nice that you allow people to defile your ears. It is not courteous to allow people who keep talking foolishness to keep talking to you. That is not courtesy. That is jeopardy and is dangerous to your God-given purpose in the earth.

Proverbs 14:7 tells you to go from the presence of a foolish man who is foolish, the one you do not perceive in him the lips of knowledge. This is the Bible's instruction of avoiding strife. The Apostle Paul writes in James 3:16 that if you open yourself to strife and bitter envy, you will be confused, and all kind of evil works will invade your purpose in God.

James 3:16 states, *"16For where envy and self-seeking exist, confusion and every evil thing are there."*

Many born-again believers are confused and cannot hear from God or be blessed because they open themselves to strife. They cannot hear clear direction from God because they have not learned to avoid strife; they have not understood the danger in strife. The word of God will affect you whether or not you know it. You don't have to know it to affect you. That is why the bible says in Hosea 4:6, "My people are destroyed for lack of knowledge."

In this kingdom, what you don't know can destroy you. Were it not for the grace of God, many would have been destroyed. The Bible is showing us that a great deal of strife is caused by communication, conversation, what we expose ourselves to, and what we use to entertain ourselves.

14

REDISCOVERING THE USE OF THE TONGUE

James 3:10–11 says, "[10] Out of the same mouth proceed blessing and cursing. My brethren, these things ought not to be so. Does a spring send forth fresh water and bitter from the same opening?" Even though blessings and cursing is coming from the same opening, they do not come from the same source. It is coming through the same opening, but it is not coming out from the same source. One set of words is coming from one source, and another set of words is coming from a different source. You let your one opening be used by both sources. Born-again believers must stop allowing an alien spirit from using their openings. The point is that when you are speaking words of discord and strife, you are speaking from an alien source.

When I bless God with my mouth and curse my brother with the same mouth, those two different utterances are coming from two different sources. I have just allowed my vessel to be used by God and the enemy. When I speak ill of my brother, I am allowing the enemy to use my vessel to curse what God has blessed, which is an abomination to God. When I gossip or speak ill of my sister, I am allowing the enemy to use my vessel.

Man tames the tongue by rediscovering its purpose. God's main purpose for creating the tongue was not for communication; neither was your mouth created for eating. When you and I understand that our mouths were not created to eat, and that our tongues weren't made to communicate, then we can hold our peace—yes, we can hold our tongues.

15

GOD FUNCTIONS BY CREATING AND BRINGING FORTH

You were created after or in the image of God. You were created to function like God or the way God functions. How does God function? God functions by creating and bringing forth. Let's see an example of how God functions in Genesis 1:1–3.

> "In the beginning God created the heavens and the earth. [2] The earth was without form, and void; and darkness was] on the face of the deep. And the Spirit of God was hovering over the face of the waters. [3] Then God said, "Let there be light" and there was light."

The Hebrew translation reads, "Then God said Light be, and light was."

God is speaking, and there is nobody there to hear Him speak. That means God's words are not for communication with somebody else; He is not speaking to be heard. God's objective of speaking is not communicating, but creation. God's objective of speaking is to bring forth, not to communicate. Your tongue was created for creation, not for communication.

When you speak what you don't want to be, you are misusing the vessel or tool you were given to create. The reason why strife and envy is so diabolical is because you are bringing forth what you don't want. You are speaking to something else that you don't want to receive. We enter into strife and envy because we do not understand our tongues were given not to communicate, but to create. Your tongue was given to you to create, not to communicate. Now you can communicate with the tongue what you want to create. You should only communicate what you want to create. You have always thought you should speak with the tongue to communicate. It is no surprise we have not been getting the results we want because we have not been using our tongues correctly. We have been using our tongues for the wrong purpose. Abnormal use of the tongue results in confusion and all kinds of evil work. Abnormal use of the tongue is called abuse. That is why when you speak ill of somebody, it is called verbal abuse.

The scripture gives us examples of the Godhead functioning to create and bring forth.

The Father

The Father did everything by speaking to create and calling or bringing forth into existence. We are to call those things that are not as though they were. Genesis 1:6 says,"[6]Then God said, 'Firmament be in the midst of the waters, and divide the waters from the waters.'"

Genesis 1:9 states, "[9]Then God said, 'waters under the heavens be gathered together into one place, and dry land appear'; and it was so."

Genesis 1:11 says, "Then God said, "Earth bring forth grass, the herb that yields seed, and the fruit tree that yields fruit according to its kind, whose seed is in itself, on the earth"; and it was so."

Genesis 1:14 says, "[14]Then God said, 'Lights be in the firmament of the heavens to divide the day from the night; and be for signs and seasons, and for days and years.'"

Genesis 1:20 states, "Then God said, 'Waters abound with an abundance of living creatures, and let birds fly above the earth across the face of the firmament of the heavens.'"

Genesis 1:24 says, "²⁴Then God said, 'Earth bring forth the living creature according to its kind: cattle and creeping thing and beast of the earth, *each* according to its kind'; and it was so."

Genesis 1:26–27 adds, "Then God said, 'Let Us make man in Our image, according to Our likeness; Let him use his tongue and his word to bring forth and create.'"

God is eternal, and whatever He creates and brings forth is eternal. Likewise, man is eternal and is supposed to create and bring forth eternal, godly things. This is why the confession of God's word is a powerful thing, because I am not speaking to be heard. This why declaration of the word of God is a powerful thing, because I am not speaking to be heard. I am speaking to bring forth and to create. Men! when you get this revelation, it will lit you up. You will kneel down on your knees, lifting up your hands, and telling God, "Please forgive me. I have been abusing my vessel for creation and bringing forth. I have not been using it for the right purpose. From now I will use it to create and to bring forth your purpose."

Your tongue is not for blessing and cursing — it is only for blessing. Your tongue is for bringing forth. Your tongue is not for communication; it is for creation. You may communicate with it, but you should only communicate what you want to create; that will shut down strife. You can start recreating your world right from where you are, You can start now recreating your environment. You can now create your own world. The Bible declares by faith the worlds were framed by the word of God.

Hebrews 11:3 says, "By faith we understand that the worlds were framed by the word of God, so that the things which are seen were not made of things which are visible." God created the world He wanted by what He said. He created you in His image and created what you want by what you say. Start saying the things you want, and they will come forth; they will manifest. That is how you are supposed to manifest God's character, nature, and authority on earth. That is who you are.

The Son

Like the Father, Jesus spoke and acted similarly to the Father to create and to bring forth. Jesus heals two blind men by touching and speaking and agreeing with their faith. Matthew 9:29 says, "Jesus touched their eyes, saying, 'According to your faith let it be to you.'"

Jesus heals a mute man possessed by a demon by speaking, rebuking the foul spirit, and speaking healing. Mark 9:25 states, "When Jesus saw that the people came running together, He rebuked the unclean spirit, saying to it: 'Deaf and dumb spirit, I command you, come out of him and enter him no more!'"

Jesus heals a leper by touching and speaking cleansing and healing to him. Mark 1:41 says, "⁴¹ Then Jesus, moved with compassion, stretched out His hand

and touched him, and said to him, 'I am willing; be cleansed.'"

Jesus heals a paralytic by agreeing with the faith of the friends and speaking forgiveness to him. Mark 2:5 says, "When Jesus saw their faith, He said to the paralytic, 'Son, your sins are forgiven you.'"

Jesus heals a woman with internal bleeding, agreeing with her faith and speaking peace and healing to her. Mark 5:34 states, "And He said to her, 'Daughter, your faith has made you well. Go in peace, and be healed of your affliction.'"

At Jesus's word, Peter catches a great number of fish. Luke 5:4–6 says, "⁴ When He had stopped speaking, He said to Simon, 'Launch out into the deep and let down your nets for a catch.' ⁵ But Simon answered and said to Him, 'Master, we have toiled all night and caught nothing;

nevertheless at Your word I will let down the net.' [6]And when they had done this, they caught a great number of fish, and their net was breaking."

Jesus raises a widow's son by touching and speaking life to the dead son. Luke 7:14 says, "Then He came and touched the open coffin, and those who carried him stood still. And He said, 'Young man, I say to you, arise.'"

Jesus heals a man with a withered hand by instructing him to stretch his hand by faith. Matthew 12:13 says, "Then He said to the man, 'Stretch out your hand.' And he stretched it out, and it was restored as whole as the other."

Jesus calms a stormy sea by speaking peace to it. Mark 4:39 relates, "Then He arose and rebuked the wind, and said to the sea,

'Peace, be still!' And the wind ceased and there was a great calm."

Jesus raises a dead damsel from the dead by touching and speaking life to her. Luke 8:54 says, "But He put them all outside, took her by the hand and called, saying, 'Little girl, arise.'"

Jesus heals a man who was crippled for [38]thirty-eight years by instructing him to do by faith those thing he does not do. John 5:8 says, "Jesus said to him, 'Rise, take up your bed and walk.'"

Jesus heals a woman with infirmity for eighteen years by speaking and loosing her from her infirmity. Luke 13:12 states, "But when Jesus saw her, He called her to Him and said to her, 'Woman, you are loosed from your infirmity.'"

Jesus resurrects Lazarus from the dead by bringing him forth. John 11:43 says,

"Now when He had said these things, He cried with a loud voice, 'Lazarus, come forth!'"

Jesus casts out demon by speaking and rebuking it. Luke 4:35 tells us, "But Jesus rebuked him, saying, 'Be quiet, and come out of him!' And when the demon had thrown him in their midst, it came out of him and did not hurt him."

The Apostles

The Father and the Son gave power to the born-again Christian to forgive sins, heal the sick, cast out devils, and bless.

Genesis 1:28 says, "Then God blessed them, and God said to them, 'Be fruitful and multiply; fill the earth and subdue it; have dominion over the fish of the sea, over the birds of the air, and over every living thing that moves on the earth.'"

Genesis 12:2 says, "I will make you a great nation; I will bless you And make your name great; And you shall be a blessing."

Genesis 22:17 declares, "Blessing I will bless you, and multiplying I will multiply your descendants as the stars of the heaven and as the sand which is on the seashore; and your descendants shall possess the gate of their enemies."

Genesis 28:4 states, "And give you the blessing of Abraham, To you and your descendants with you, That you may inherit the land In which you are a stranger, Which God gave to Abraham."

Romans 4:13 says, "The Promise Granted Through Faith For the promise that he would be the heir of the world was not to Abraham or to his seed through the law, but through the righteousness of faith."

Romans 4:16 says, "Therefore it is of faith that it might be according to grace, so that the promise might be sure to all the seed, not only to those who are of the law, but also to those who are of the faith of Abraham, who is the father of us all."

Galatians 3:9 tells us, "So then those who *are* of faith are blessed with believing Abraham."

Galatians 3:16 states, "Now to Abraham and his Seed were the promises made. He does not say, 'And to seeds,' as of many, but as of one, 'And to your Seed,' who is Christ."

Galatians 3:29 says, "And if you *are* Christ's, then you are Abraham's seed, and heirs according to the promise."

Hebrews 2:16 says, "For indeed He does not give aid to angels, but He does give aid to the seed of Abraham."

John 20:21–23 says, "²¹ So Jesus said to them again, 'Peace to you! As the Father has sent Me, I also send you.' ²² And when He had said this, He breathed on them, and said to them, 'Receive the Holy Spirit. ²³If you forgive the sins of any, they are forgiven them; if you retain the sins of any, they are retained.'"

Luke 10:19 states, "Behold, I give you the authority to trample on serpents and scorpions, and over all the power of the enemy, and nothing shall by any means hurt you."

These promises are to God and should manifest in the life and ministry of the Christian. God's power and blessing should manifest in the life and ministry of the Christian. Jesus introduced and trained His disciples in the areas of signs, wonders, and miracles. They saw the dead raised, the lepers cleansed, a small food supply multiplied to feed a multitude, and many other phenomenal sights. They were recommissioned to go out under Jesus's authority and name and announce the kingdom of God to the Jewish people via demonstration of His power.

John 14:12 says, "Most assuredly, I say to you, he who believes in Me, the works that I do he will do also, and greater works than these he will do, because I go to My Father." The apostles took the challenge and started to function like the Father and the Son.

Peter and John heal lame man by speaking by faith calling healing to come forth. Acts 3:6 says, "Then Peter said, 'Silver and gold I do not have, but what I do have I give you: In the name of Jesus Christ of Nazareth, rise up and walk.'"

Peter raises Dorcus from the dead by calling forth life into her. Acts 9:40-41 says "⁴⁰But Peter put them all out, and knelt down and prayed. And turning to the body he said, 'Tabitha, arise.'" And she opened her eyes, and when she saw Peter she sat up. Then he gave her *his* hand and lifted her up; and when he had called the saints and widows, he presented her alive"

You can shake of the place of prayer by praying the word. Acts 4:31 says, "And when they had prayed, the place where they were assembled together was shaken; and they were all filled with the Holy Spirit, and they spoke the word of God with boldness."

Regarding speaking in tongues, Acts 2:6–8 states, "And when this sound occurred, the multitude came together, and were confused, because everyone heard them speak in his own language. [7]Then they were all amazed and marveled, saying to one another, 'Look, are not all these who speak Galileans? [8] And how *is it that* we hear, each in our own language in which we were born?"

There were many miracles by the apostles. Acts 2:43 says, "Then fear came upon every soul, and many wonders and signs were done through the apostles."

Mass Healing's by the Apostles.

Acts 5:15–16 states, "[15] So that they brought the sick out into the streets and laid *them* on beds and couches, that at least the shadow of Peter passing by might fall on some of them. [16] Also a multitude gathered from the surrounding cities to Jerusalem, bringing sick people and those who were tormented by unclean spirits, and they were all healed."

Stephen operated by faith and power in his ministry, and he did great wonders and signs among the people. Acts 6:8 says, "And Stephen, full of faith and power, did great wonders and signs among the people."

Philip at Samaria healed multitudes, paralytics, and the lame. Acts 8:5–8 says, "[5] Then Philip went down to the city of Samaria and preached Christ to them. [6]And the multitudes with one accord heeded the things spoken by Philip, hearing and seeing the miracles which he did. [7] For unclean spirits, crying with a loud voice, came out of many who were possessed; and many who were paralyzed and lame were healed. [8] And there was great joy in that city."

Peter heals Aeneas by speaking and instructing him. Acts 9:34 says, "And Peter said to him, 'Aeneas, Jesus the

Christ heals you. Arise and make your bed.' Then he arose immediately."

Now let us look at some words of our Lord Jesus the Christ in this context. Matthew 12:31–37 says,

> "Therefore I say to you, every sin and blasphemy will be forgiven men, but the blasphemy against the Spirit will not be forgiven men. [32]Anyone who speaks a word against the Son of Man, it will be forgiven him; but whoever speaks against the Holy Spirit, it will not be forgiven him, either in this age or in the age to come. [33] "Either make the tree good and its fruit good, or else make the tree bad and its fruit bad; for a tree is known by its fruit. [34]Brood of vipers! How can you, being evil, speak good things? For out of the abundance of the heart the mouth speaks. [35] A good man out of the

good treasure of his heart brings forth good things, and an evil man out of the evil treasure brings forth evil things. [36]But I say to you that for every idle word men may speak, they will give account of it in the day of judgment. [37]For by your words you will be justified, and by your words you will be condemned."

You can only speak from the source that is within you. Verse 33 says, "Either make the tree good and its fruit good, or else make the tree bad and its fruit bad; for a tree is known by its fruit." What you speak is what is in you, and that is what is coming out. I am not tripping you because I know you are a bad tree right now. I have come to change the tree in you. He was not condemning them and telling them they were going to hell. He was telling them right now the only thing in them was hell. Your tongue is set on fire by hell.

Verse 34 says, "[34]Brood of vipers! How can you, being evil, speak good things? For out of the abundance of the heart the mouth speaks." Jesus is telling them, "I am a good tree and am bringing forth good fruit. You are bad tree and are bringing forth bad fruit. I have come to change your tree in you." Jesus says, "Out of the abundance of the heart, the mouth speaks."

Verses 35–37 cover legal matters. If you are justified in a court of law, you are acquitted because you are not guilty; you are released. Therefore by your words you have a release, by your words you will be condemned, and by your words you will be incarcerated. You are getting a release or incarceration by what you are saying.

This is not religion, but it is a spiritual law of creation.

Jesus was speaking to people who were not born again; that was why they were bringing forth bad fruit. James was speaking to people who were born again, telling them, "You have now been born again. You should not be bringing forth bad fruit. The good tree is in you, and you have a choice of what you bring forth."

Proverbs 18:21 states, "Death and life are in the power of the tongue, and those who love it will eat its fruit." If you love life, you will eat of it by speaking it. If you love death, you will eat of it by speaking it.

Deuteronomy 11:26 says, "Behold, I set before you today a blessing and a curse." God set before them life or death by their tongues. God is not choosing who lives and who dies. He is not determining who is released to prosperity and who is incarcerated in debt.

Do not say that you are doing the word when your words defy your actions. God is not talking of killing people. He is cutting down the evil tree that was planted in you in the garden. Another fountain was opened to the human race in the garden when man transgressed. It was another source of information and revelation that was not coming from God. That is why when God came to Adam, Adam said, "I am naked." God said, "I never said that, I never called you naked! Why are you letting that come out of your mouth? That is not from me!" There must now be another source, plant, or tree that is causing death. From that time until Jesus came, men learned to speak from that source. That is why it took hundreds of years to learn to die, because they were not educated in speaking death.

It took hundreds of years to learn to kill themselves with their words. We read of men like Methuselah who lived 969 years. God cut man's longevity of life to 120 years because man continued speaking death rather than life.

Genesis 6:3 says, "And the LORD said, 'My Spirit shall not strive with man forever, for he is indeed flesh; yet his days shall be one hundred and twenty years.'"

Genesis 5 is the book of the genealogy of Adam.

> [5] So all the days that Adam lived were Nine Hundred And Thirty years
>
> [8] So all the days of Seth were Nine Hundred And Twelve years
>
> [11] So all the days of Enosh were Nine Hundred And Five years

[14] So all the days of Cainan were Nine Hundred And Ten years

[17] So all the days of Mahalalel were Eight Hundred And Ninety-Five years

[20] So all the days of Jared were Nine Hundred And Sixty-Two years

[23] So all the days of Enoch were Three Hundred And Sixty-Five years

[27] So all the days of Methuselah were Nine Hundred And Sixty-Nine years

[31] So all the days of Lamech were Seven Hundred And Seventy-Seven years.

Genesis 9:29 states, "So all the days of Noah were nine hundred and fifty years; and he died."

Genesis 11:10–11 adds, "This *is* the genealogy of Shem: Shem *was* one hundred years old, and begot Arphaxad two years after the flood. After he begot Arphaxad, Shem lived five hundred years, and begot sons and daughters. The days of Shem were six hundred years."

Genesis 25:7 says, "This *is* the sum of the years of Abraham's life which he lived: one hundred and seventy-five years."

Genesis 6:3 states,… "My Spirit shall not strive with man forever, for he *is* indeed flesh; yet his days shall be one hundred and twenty years."

Psalm 90:10 says, "The days of our lives *are* seventy years; And if by reason of strength *they are* eighty years, Yet their boast *is* only labor and sorrow; For it is soon cut off, and we fly away."

Genesis 6:1–7 shows the process of shortening of man's longevity of life, all because of speaking death rather than life to himself.

Matthew 3:11 says, "I indeed baptize you with water to repentance. But he that comes after me is mightier than I, whose shoes I am not worthy to bear. He shall baptize you with the Holy Ghost, and with fire."

Jesus came to cut down that tree. He means to immerse you into something else, where you relearn to speak life. Proverbs 18:21 states, "Death and life are in the power of the tongue." Now no human can tame the tongue, but that baptism will tame the tongue. The Holy Spirit will tame the tongue. The word of God will tame the tongue.

John 1:1 says, "In the beginning was the Word, and the Word was with God, and the Word was God."

God and His word are one. When the word tames the tongue, it is God who tames the tongue. When you learn to speak in line with the word, you are taming the tongue. The meditation of the word of God—not the reading of it, but the meditation of it—tames the tongue. The reading and memorization of God's word only affects the intellect. Memorization is an intellectual exercise. Meditation is a special exercise of the soul.

The word *meditation* means to mutter, repeat, or go over. Proverbs 22:18 says, "For it is a pleasant thing if you keep them within you; Let them all be fixed upon your lips." That means if the words of God are established (dwell constantly) upon your lips, they "keep the door of your lips" against sin, teaching you what to say and how to speak without fear, even before kings. The "praises of God" will forever be in his mouth. The promise of the word of God is that it will be fitted on your lips. God says, "When you meditate on my Word I will fit it in your mouth whenever you need it."

The equivalent in the New Testament is in John 14:26. "But the Helper, the Holy Spirit, whom the Father will send in My name, He will teach you all things, and bring to your remembrance all things that I said to you." You don't try to remember it, but you let Him speak to you. The Holy Spirit will bring it to your remembrance.

If you get the word of God in your mouth and submit your tongue to the Holy Spirit, you will not be able to curse your brother or sister and bless God. You will not be able to speak ill of your brother or sister and yet also bless God. This is the other reason praying in the Spirit is a spiritual exercise that tames the tongue. When you pray in the Holy Spirit, your spirit is praying.

First Corinthians 14:14 says, "For if I pray in a tongue, my spirit prays, but my understanding is unfruitful." That is important because my spirit is indwelt by the Holy Spirit. His Spirit bears witness with mine; I am spirit, and the Holy Spirit is in me. If my spirit is praying, I am praying in the Holy Spirit. The Holy Spirit now has control over my tongue.

All of us have learned the discipline of allowing our intellects to use our tongues. We have gained the ability to control the tongue. When you pray in the Spirit, your spirit is utilizing your tongue. In any other realm regarding the use of your tongue, your intellect and mind are using it. Your tongue can only speak what your mind can conceive, because your intellect is using your tongue. An educated mind without an illuminated spirit is equivalent to bringing forth evil. I don't understand why you would be surprised when intelligent people bring forth evil; they are most qualified to bring forth evil. That is why if the light in you is darkness, how great is that darkness. The more educated you get without illumination, the greater the darkness. The more intellectual people are without illumination, the greater the capacity they have to do evil, and they bring it forth by the tongue. Social media is potentially one of the most wicked things that has been introduced in the twenty-first century. Why should we even wonder about cyberbullying? It is simply the use of intellect to transmit words of power and of death. The enemy has a greater capacity to transmit words. You need to understand what you are doing when you use words.

Remember this: your tongue was created not for communication but for creation. You communicate what you want to create. Oh, if only we can remember that our minds can be renewed to the truth and that our tongues were designed to create. When I really get upset with you, I would bless you. You will understand why Jesus said, "Bless those who curse you," not because you feel like doing it but because you want them blessed.

Proverbs 18:8 states, "The words of a talebearer are like tasty trifles, and they go down into the inmost body."

Those words go down into the body and bring cancer, depression, suicidal thoughts, low self-esteem, and more.

When you understand what the tongue was designed to do and accept the word of God, your mind will stop using your tongue as a weapon. Our tongues are not meant to sow strife and discord; they are meant to speak and release blessing.

Genesis 11 is the situation at the Tower of Babel. The people had one language and one mind, and their words were in line with one another. When they were in this tight agreement, nothing was withheld from what they wanted to do. In their mouths, they had the power to bring forth. God came down and confused their language because they were going to create what was undesirable. God had placed such power on the man to bring forth and create. Their words were not in line with the word of God.

God has placed such power on man to bring forth and create so that if people keep speaking in line with the word of God, they will keep understanding and agreeing with one another. Ultimately, they will manifest anything they want. That is the power of speaking in agreement. If you understand that power, you will use your tongue with greater discipline. If you don't want to bring forth, don't say it. If you don't want it to be, then don't speak it. If you want it to come to a stop, then stop speaking about it. Stop lighting the fire with your tongue.

Declaration

Father, I declare my best days are with me. I speak blessing into my tomorrow. I speak favor into my tomorrow. I speak increase, multiplication, and replenishment. Lord, You delight in the prosperity of Your servant. I speak prosperity into my weekend, my next week, my next month, the years to come, and into my future. I decree favor to meet me tomorrow. Lord, I declare You surround me with faithful men and women, trustworthy friends men and women who will encourage my faith and strengthen me in the things of God.